A Kid's Guide to Managing Time

A Children's Book about Using Time Efficiently and Effectively

by

Joy Wilt

Illustrated by Ernie Hergenroeder

Educational Products Division
Word, Incorporated
Waco, Texas

Author

JOY WILT is creator and director of Children's Ministries, an organization that provides resources "for people who care about children"—speakers, workshops, demonstrations, consulting services, and training institutes. A certified elementary school teacher, administrator, and early childhood specialist, Joy is also consultant to and professor in the master's degree program in children's ministries for Fuller Theological Seminary. Joy is a graduate of LaVerne College, LaVerne, California (B.A. in Biological Science), and Pacific Oaks College, Pasadena, California (M.A. in Human Development). She is author of three books, *Happily Ever After, An Uncomplicated Guide to Becoming a Superparent,* and *Taming the Big Bad Wolves,* as well as the popular *Can-Make-And-Do Books.* Joy's commitment "never to forget what it feels like to be a child" permeates the many innovative programs she has developed and her work as lecturer, consultant, writer, and—not least—mother of two children, Christopher and Lisa.

Artist

ERNIE HERGENROEDER is founder and owner of Hergie & Associates (a visual communications studio and advertising agency). With the establishment of this company in 1975, "Hergie" and his wife, Faith, settled in San Jose with their four children, Lynn, Kathy, Stephen, and Beth. Active in community and church affairs, Hergie is involved in presenting creative workshops for teachers, ministers, and others who wish to understand the techniques of communicating visually. He also lectures in high schools to encourage young artists toward a career in commercial art. Hergie serves as a consultant to organizations such as the Police Athletic League (PAL), Girl Scouts, and religious and secular corporations. His ultimate goal is to touch the hearts of kids (8 to 80) all over the world—visually!

ISBN: 0-8499-8139-5
Library of Congress Catalog Card Number: 79-51585
Janet Gray, Editor

Contents

Introduction

A Kid's Guide to Managing Time is one of a series of books. The complete set is called *Ready-Set-Grow!*

A Kid's Guide to Managing Time deals with time management and can be used by itself or as part of a program that utilizes all of the *Ready-Set-Grow!* books.

A Kid's Guide to Managing Time is specifically designed so that children can either read the book themselves or have it read to them. This can be done at home, church, or school. When reading to children, it is not necessary to complete the book at one sitting. Concern should be given to the attention span of the individual child and his or her comprehension of the subject matter.

A Kid's Guide to Managing Time is designed to involve the child in the concepts that are being taught. This is done by simply and carefully explaining each concept and then asking questions that invite a response from the child. It is hoped that by answering the questions the child will personalize the concept and, thus, integrate it into his or her thinking.

Everyone has the same amount of time in a day, a week, a year. What makes a difference is how people use their time. Much of a child's time is structured by others. Believing his or her time to be out of his or her own control can be very frustrating to a child and can cause him or her actually to waste the time he or she could spend doing things he or she enjoys.

A Kid's Guide to Managing Time helps a child plan what he or she needs and wants to do on a yearly, monthly, weekly, and daily basis. It offers tips for getting through the unpleasant tasks that must be done so that the child can take time to do the things he or she chooses to do. It explains when watching television, socializing, and "goofing off" are escapes from responsibility, and when they are healthy ways a child can relax and reward himself or herself for a job well done.

A Kid's Guide to Managing Time is designed to teach children the importance of thinking about how they spend their time and using it wisely, so they can control it to accomplish goals that are fulfilling to them. This is important because time is what life is made of. As people grow older, they understand better how precious God's gift of time is, and all too often regret how much time they have wasted. Children who learn early how to manage their time will be better equipped to live happy, fulfilling lives.

A Kid's Guide to Managing Time

No matter who you are, time is an important part of your life.

If you are like most people your age, you get up at a certain time each morning.

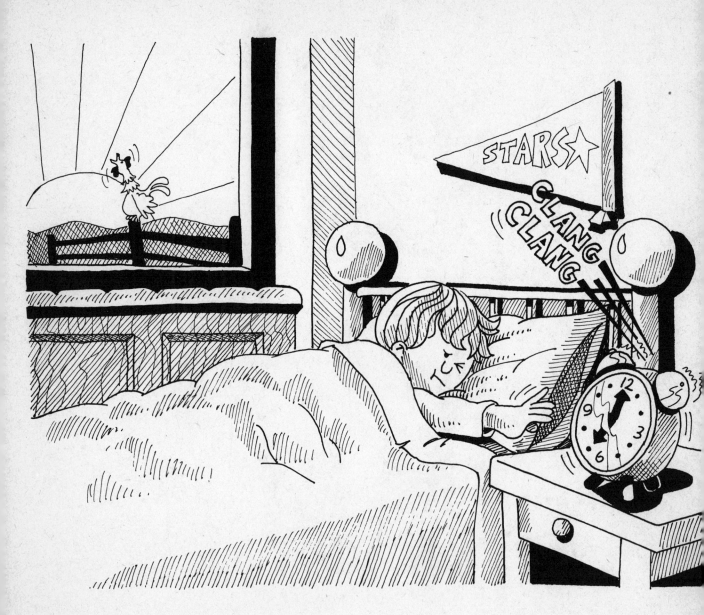

You eat at a certain time.

You go to bed at a certain time.

Time is an important part of your life. Do you know what it is?

Chapter 1

What Is Time?

Time is when things happen.

Time is what a clock shows.

A clock shows . . .

A second is about the amount of time it takes you to say, "One chimpanzee."

THIS IS THE SECOND HAND.

Not all clocks have a second hand, but on the ones that do, the second hand is the hand that moves the fastest. It moves from one number to the next in five seconds, and it goes all the way around the clock every minute.

A minute is sixty seconds.

THIS IS THE MINUTE HAND.

The long hand on the clock is the minute hand. It moves from one number to the next in five minutes, and it goes all the way around the clock every hour.

An hour is sixty minutes.

THIS IS THE HOUR HAND.

The short hand on the clock is the hour hand. It moves from one number to the next in one hour, and it goes all the way around the clock every twelve hours.

Time is also what a calendar shows.

A calendar shows . . .

DAYS,
WEEKS,
MONTHS,
and
YEARS.

A day lasts twenty-four hours. It begins at twelve o'clock midnight. It has a morning, a noon, an afternoon, an evening, and then it ends again at midnight.

The hour hand goes all the way around the clock twice during a day. The twelve hours from midnight (when the day begins) to noon are called a.m. The twelve hours from noon to midnight (when the day ends) are called p.m.

A week is seven days:

Sunday,

Monday,

Tuesday,

Wednesday,

Thursday,

Friday, and

Saturday.

There are just over four weeks in a month.

Each day of the month is shown as a number on the calendar.

Some months have 30 days. Other months have 31 days. February has 28 days, except during leap year, when it has 29 days. Leap year happens every four years.

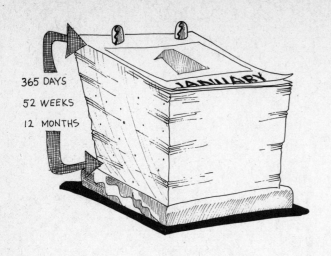

365 DAYS
52 WEEKS
12 MONTHS

In a year, there are:

365 days,

52 weeks, and

12 months.

The months are:

January,	July,
February,	August,
March,	September,
April,	October,
May,	November,
June,	December.

A year has four seasons.

The first season, winter, starts in December and lasts through
January and February.

The second season, spring, starts in March and lasts through
April and May.

The third season, summer, starts in June and lasts through July and August.

The fourth season, fall, starts in September and lasts through November.

Time has a past, a present, and a future.

The past is the time that has already happened.

The present is the time right now.

The future is all the time to come.

YOU USED TO BE A BABY.
THAT'S IN THE PAST.
DINOSAURS LIVED EVEN
FARTHER BACK IN THE
PAST. YESTERDAY IS IN
THE PAST, TOO, AND SO IS
FIVE MINUTES AGO.
THIS VERY MINUTE IS THE
PRESENT.

SOME DAY YOU'LL BE
A GROWNUP, AND MAYBE
YOU'LL BE ABLE TO GO TO
THE MOON ON VACATION.
THAT'S IN THE FUTURE.
TOMORROW'S
IN THE FUTURE,
TOO.

PAST

PRESENT

FUTURE

MOON

Time never stops.

Time never slows down.

Time never speeds up.

Everyone, no matter who he or she is, gets the same number of seconds, minutes, and hours in every day, and everyone gets the same number of days, weeks, and months in every year.

But no two people use time in exactly the same way.

Some people use their time wisely. Others waste it.

What do you do with your time?

The next chapter will help you answer this question.

Chapter 2

How Do You Spend Your Time?

Everyone spends time sleeping.

Everyone spends time eating.

Most people spend time either at work or in school.

Most people spend some time doing things that must be done.

And most people spend time playing and relaxing.

What do you spend your time doing? There's a way you can figure this out.

You can begin by making two time charts.

Make one chart that looks like this:

TIME	SUNDAY	MONDAY
MIDNIGHT TO 1:00 A.M.		
1:00 — 2:00 A.M.		
2:00 — 3:00 A.M.		
3:00 — 4:00 A.M.		
4:00 — 5:00 A.M.		
5:00 — 6:00 A.M.		
6:00 — 7:00 A.M.		
7:00 — 8:00 A.M.		
8:00 — 9:00 A.M.		
9:00 — 10:00 A.M.		
10:00 — 11:00 A.M.		
11:00 — 12:00 NOON		
NOON — 1:00 P.M.		
1:00 — 2:00 P.M.		
2:00 — 3:00 P.M.		
3:00 — 4:00 P.M.		
4:00 — 5:00 P.M.		
5:00 — 6:00 P.M.		
6:00 — 7:00 P.M.		
7:00 — 8:00 P.M.		
8:00 — 9:00 P.M.		
9:00 — 10:00 P.M.		
10:00 — 11:00 P.M.		
11:00 P.M. — MIDNIGHT		

CHART # 1

TUESDAY	WEDNESDAY	THURSDAY	FRIDAY	SATURDAY

Make the other chart look like this:

ACTIVITY	TIME TOTAL HOURS		
	SUNDAY	MONDAY	TUESDAY

CHART #2
SPENT EACH DAY

WEDNESDAY	THURSDAY	FRIDAY	SATURDAY	TOTAL HOURS SPENT ALL WEEK

Beginning on a Sunday, use Time Chart # 1 to keep track of how you spend your time each day for a week. To do this, take a few minutes once or twice a day to write a few words about what you have done each hour. For instance, from midnight to seven or eight o'clock on Sunday morning, you were probably sleeping, so write "Sleeping" in each box for that time period.

TIME	SUNDAY	MONDAY	TUESDAY	WEDNESDAY	THURSDAY	FRIDAY	SATURDAY
MIDNIGHT TO 1:00 AM	SLEEPING						
1:00 — 2:00 A.M.	SLEEPING						
2:00 — 3:00 A.M.	SLEEPING						
3:00 — 4:00 A.M.	SLEEPING						
4:00 — 5:00 A.M.	SLEEPING						
5:00 — 6:00 A.M.	SLEEPING						
6:00 — 7:00 A.M.	SLEEPING						
7:00 — 8:00 A.M.							
8:00 — 9:00 A.M.							
9:00 — 10:00 A.M.							
10:00 — 11:00 A.M.							
11:00 — 12:00 NOON							
NOON — 1:00 P.M.							
1:00 — 2:00 P.M.							
2:00 — 3:00 P.M.							
3:00 — 4:00 P.M.							
4:00 — 5:00 P.M.							
5:00 — 6:00 P.M.							
6:00 — 7:00 P.M.							
7:00 — 8:00 P.M.							
8:00 — 9:00 P.M.							
9:00 — 10:00 P.M.							
10:00 — 11:00 P.M.							
11:00 P.M. — MIDNIGHT							

TIME CHART # 1

ACTIVITY	TIME CHART #2 TOTAL HOURS SPENT EACH DAY							TOTAL HOURS SPENT ALL WEEK
	SUNDAY	MONDAY	TUESDAY	WEDNESDAY	THURSDAY	FRIDAY	SATURDAY	
SLEEPING	9 HRS.	9 HRS.	9 HRS.	9 HRS.	9 HRS.	9 HRS.	9 HRS.	63 HRS.
SCHOOL		5 HRS.	5 HRS.	5 HRS.	5 HRS.	5 HRS.		25 HRS.
PLAYING								
HOMEWORK								
CHORES								

After you've finished Time Chart # 1, use it to fill out Time Chart # 2. To do this, list in the column headed "Activity" each thing you did during the week, such as sleeping, playing, homework, and chores. For each activity, add up how much time you spent doing it each day, and fill in the spaces under "Total Hours Spent Each Day." Then add up the total hours you spent on each activity all week and fill in the total in the last column.

49

After you have completed both charts, study them carefully.

Ask yourself these questions.

What did I spend the most time doing?

What did I spend the least time doing?

Is there something I would like to have spent more time doing?

Is there something I would like to have spent less time doing?

Is there something I would like to have done, but didn't do?

Did I have enough free time when I could do whatever I wanted to do?

Did I get to spend enough time doing things I decided to do?

Do I feel good about the way I spent my time?

If you are like most people your age, you will probably discover that you spend a great deal of time asleep or at school. Whether you like this or not, you probably don't have much control over it.

But you probably do have some control over the time when you are not asleep or at school.

What do you do with the time you have left over after sleeping and going to school? Do you do the things you need to do? Do you do the things you want to do?

The next chapter will tell you how you can get in control of your time, so you can do all the things you need and want to do.

Chapter 3

Planning Your Time

There are certain things you need to do in order to stay alive
and grow—things like eating, sleeping, and . . .

going to school.

Then there are the things you want to do—things that are fun, exciting, and satisfying.

Both the things you need to do and the things you want to do are important.

Some of the things you need or want to do can be done in a day, others can be done in a week, while others take a month or a year.

Because this is true, you may want to have:

DAILY plans for what you hope to get done during a day,

WEEKLY plans for what you hope to get done during a week,

MONTHLY plans for what you hope to get done during a month, and

ANNUAL plans for what you hope to get done during a year.

Planning what you do with your time is one of the most important things you can do.

Here is a list of equipment you will need to do a good job of planning:

a large sheet of poster paper,

a calendar with spaces large enough to write in for each day,

a pencil,

an eraser,

a tablet of blank paper, and

a watch (if possible).

You do not have to make plans for everything you do every day. You do some things automatically—things like dressing, eating, going to school, bathing, and sleeping.

I ALREADY KNOW I'M GOING TO DO THESE THINGS. WHAT ELSE SHALL I DO?

When you're making your plans, you can allow time for these things, but you don't have to make special plans to do them.

January 1, the first day of the year, is a good time to start planning for a year. So is the first day of school. But you can start any time.

Here are four steps you can take in making your plans.

STEP 1: ASK YOURSELF:

What do I need to do this year?
What do I want to do this year?

Do I want to:

Get something? What?
Become something? What?

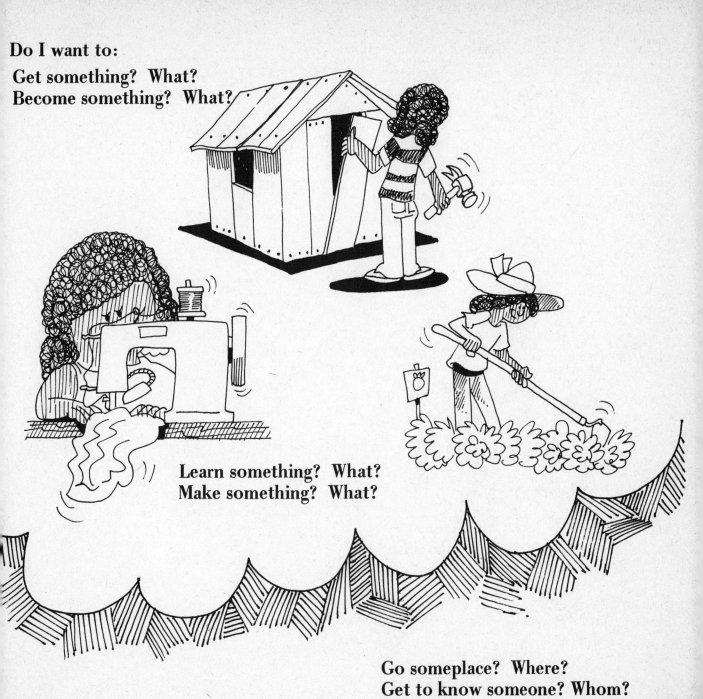

Learn something? What?
Make something? What?

Go someplace? Where?
Get to know someone? Whom?

Write down all the answers to these questions that come into your head.

I CAN'T JOIN THE BASEBALL TEAM AND THE SWIM TEAM, BECAUSE THEY BOTH PRACTICE AT THE SAME TIME. I'LL CROSS OFF THE BASEBALL TEAM. I'D LIKE TO BUILD A FORT, BUT I'D NEED HELP, AND NONE OF MY FRIENDS WANT TO BUILD ONE. SO I'LL CROSS OFF THE FORT. I'M GROWING A GARDEN AT SCHOOL, SO I REALLY DON'T NEED TO GROW ONE HERE.

* BUY A BIKE.
* ~~JOIN THE BASEBALL TEAM.~~
LEARN HOW TO SEW.
~~BUILD A FORT.~~
GO TO CAMP.
~~GROW A GARDEN.~~
JOIN THE SWIM TEAM.

STEP 3: CROSS OUT THE THINGS THAT ARE IMPOSSIBLE OR UNIMPORTANT.

To make sure your list isn't too long, go through it carefully and cross out the things you don't really want to do and the things you won't be able to do. Chances are you'll be able to cross out several things.

STEP 4: MAKE A PRIORITY LIST.

To do this, decide which of the things you've written down are most important, which are not so important, and which are least important. Put the most important things at the top of the list and the least important things at the bottom.

For your annual plans, you may want to make a chart on the large sheet of poster paper and put it up where you can see it every day. The chart will remind you of the things you want to accomplish during the year. These are your goals.

When you have made your annual plans, you're ready to start on your monthly and weekly plans. A lot of what you do during a month or a week will depend on your goals.

Look at your goals. Think about each one, and ask yourself, "What do I need to do to accomplish this goal?"

Next, make a list. Write down everything you can think of that you need to do to reach your goal.

Then, organize your list. Write down the things you need to do in the order in which they must be done.

FIRST I NEED TO GET MY PHYSICAL AND TURN IN MY PERMISSION SLIP, BECAUSE I CAN'T TRY OUT WITHOUT THOSE. THEN I NEED TO TRY OUT. IF I MAKE THE TEAM, I'LL BUY MY SUIT. THEN I'LL GO TO PRACTICE EVERY MONDAY, WEDNESDAY, AND FRIDAY.

5. GO TO P... EVERY... MONDAY, WEDNESDAY, AND FRIDAY.

Next, fill in your calendar. Write down exactly when you plan to do the things on your list.

It's a good idea to use a pencil when you write on a calendar. If your plans change, you can erase without messing up your calendar.

SEPTEMBER

SUN.	MON.	TUE.	WED.	THU.	FRI.	SAT.
1	2	3	VISIT DOCTOR 4	5	6	7
8	9	10	11	12	13	14
15	TURN IN THE PERMISSION SLIP 16	17	GO TO SWIM TEAM TRYOUTS 18	19	20	21
22	23	24	25	26	SHOP 27 FOR NEW SWIM SUIT	28
29	FIRST 30 DAY OF SWIM PRACTICE					

Also, make sure to write on your calendar anything you decide
to do with other people . . .

and anything you decide to do on your own.

After you set your annual goals and begin your weekly and monthly plans, you are ready to make your daily plans.

THINGS TO DO

1. RETURN BOOKS TO LIBRARY.

2. WASH MY HAIR.

3. BUY NEW SHOE-LACES.

4. GET LESLIE'S PRESENT.

Keep your pad of paper and your pencil handy. Any time you think of something you need or want to do, write it down on a "Things to Do" list.

Each morning, before you begin your day, look at your calendar and add the things you are supposed to do that day to your "Things to Do" list.

When you do something, cross it off your list.

At the end of the day, check your "Things to Do" list. If there's something on the list that you haven't crossed off, put it at the top of your "Things to Do" list for the next day.

Annual plans,

monthly plans,

weekly plans, and

daily plans . . .

will help you get the things done that you need and want to do . . .

if you follow through and do what you have planned.

The next chapter will give you some important ideas that will help you follow through with your plans.

Chapter 4

Doing What You Plan

If you are like most people, you will sometimes have to do things you do not want to do. You may not want to do everything on your goal chart, calendar, or "Things to Do" list.

MY BIKE'S BROKEN, SO I GUESS I'LL HAVE TO WALK TO THE LIBRARY. UGH! IT'S SO FAR! I'M JUST NOT GOING TO DO IT.

But sometimes it's necessary to do something, even when you don't want to.

Once you have decided something is important and needs to be done, you need to do it.

When you are faced with a task you do not want to do, there are several things you need to avoid doing if you want to make the task as easy as possible.

Avoid procrastinating.

This means, don't wait until later. If you have something unpleasant to do, do it as soon as you can. Get it over with so you can enjoy the things you want to do.

You will enjoy doing the things you want to do much more if you don't have to think about an unpleasant task that you should be doing.

Avoid escaping.

WATCHING TV

READING

DAYDREAMING

This means, don't try to get out of doing something you need to do by doing something else.

There are many ways people try to escape. Here are some of them.

GOOFING OFF

HIDING

TALKING WITH SOMEONE ELSE

All of these can be good things to do, but not if you use them to get out of doing something that needs to be done.

Avoid deceiving yourself and others.

Do what you say you will do. If you tell yourself or someone else you are going to do something, do it.

Losing trust is one of the worst things that can happen to a person. It's sad when a person can't be trusted by other people, but it's even sadder when a person can't trust himself or herself.

There are several ways you can help yourself make sure you do the things you say you will do.

One is to play a game with yourself. Set yourself a time limit and try to get the job done in that amount of time.

Race with the clock or with yourself.

LAST WEEK IT TOOK ME
FIFTEEN MINUTES TO
CARRY THE TRASH OUT.
I WONDER IF I CAN DO
IT IN TEN MINUTES.

Playing games with yourself can be fun, and it's good to get a job done quickly, if you can still do it well.

Another way you can help yourself get through something you don't want to do is to reward yourself.

Promise yourself that you will do something you really want to do after you've finished.

This is when watching television, reading, daydreaming, hiding, talking with someone else, and goofing off can really be OK. These are all great things to do when you're not using them to keep from doing things that need to be done.

A third way to make sure you do something that you need to do is tell a friend. Tell someone else about your unpleasant task, and ask him or her to encourage you to do it.

There are some old sayings that will be helpful for you to know as you go about doing what you've planned. One is, "Haste makes waste." This means when you hurry too much, sometimes you end up spending more time on a job.

This is because being in too much of a hurry can cause you to have accidents or make mistakes.

Another old saying is, "Anything worth doing is worth doing right." This means if you are going to take the time to do something, you should do it well. Otherwise you should not do it at all. Doing a bad job is a waste of time.

A third saying is, "One step at a time." This means whenever you
have a lot of things to do, you need to do them one at a time. Nobody
can do everything at once.

One last saying is, "First things first." This means you need to do the most important thing first, and the rest in the order of their importance.

Once you have decided what needs to be done, you need to do it . . . and do it well.

Conclusion

Time is when things happen.

Time is what a clock shows. A clock shows seconds, minutes and hours.

Time is what a calendar shows. A calendar shows days, weeks, months, and years.

Time has a past, a present, and a future.

Time never stops,

  never slows down, and

  never goes faster.

Time always stays the same.

Everyone has the same amount of time in a day, a week, a month, or a year. It's what people do with their time that makes a difference.

What do you do with your time?
Do you use it to do all the things you need and want to do?

Planning what you do with your time is one of the most important things you can do.

You will need to make . . .

annual plans,

monthly plans,

weekly plans, and

daily plans.

Once your plans are made, you need to follow through and do what you have planned.

This means that you must try not to:

procrastinate,

escape, or

deceive yourself or others.

Whenever you need to do something you don't want to do,
try these things to make it easier.

Play a game with yourself to make the job go more quickly.

Reward yourself when you are finished.

Tell a friend and ask him or her to remind you to get the
task done.

And remember these old sayings about time.

Haste makes waste.

Anything worth doing is worth doing right.

First things first.

One step at a time.

All of this is to say . . .

Think before you spend your time,

use it carefully, and

manage it wisely, because . . .

Time is what life is made of!